‘ The difference between winners and
losers is that winners tell the jokes and
losers talk about the run of the ball. ’

First published in Great Britain in 1996 by

Chameleon Books

106 Great Russell Street

London WC1B 3LJ

Copyright for text © DC Publications Ltd

All rights reserved

CIP data for this title is available from the British Library

ISBN 0 233 99056 9

Book and jacket design by Jupiter 7 Graphics Ltd

Printed in Spain by Graficas Zamudio Printek, S.A.L.

ACKNOWLEDGEMENTS:
Special thanks to Gaynor Edwards,
Mary Killingworth, Mark Peacock,
all at Generation Associates,
Michael Heatley, Ian Welch,
Paula O'Brien, Edwin Donald, Tim Hawkins,
Angus Miller, all the keen football fans across
the country who kindly supplied us with their
stories - and the man who made it all possible -
Tim Forrester.

A special thanks to Adrian Murrell and all the
lads at Allsport Picture Agency.

Dedicated to

Dan, Ellie and Joe

David Crowe

Football doesn't always follow the script - whether you're attempting to knock in a penalty in front of 70,000 in an international at Wembley, or trying to clear a cross in front of one man and a dog at the local rec, football has a way of humbling the most skilled player.

If you don't believe me have a look at the pages that follow and you'll see there are many ways to score an own goal.

Ray Wilkins, MBE

Ray Wilkins' writer's fee for this publication was donated to Help A London Child, a registered charity, at his request.

❛ Football is all very well as a game for rough girls, but it is hardly suitable for delicate boys. ❜

OSCAR WILDE

A FUNNY OLD GAME...

OVER THE WALL

WHEN I GOT demobbed out of the RAF I went down to Bramall Lane for a trial with Sheffield United.

Training with the first team was great till one day in a practice match we were playing with the old leather ball when I really did clear my line of defence. As one of the first team players was breaking away I challenged him and cleared the danger as I kicked the ball away.

The only problem was the ball not only cleared the danger it also cleared the big wall that surrounded the training pitch. I went to retrieve it, but it was not in the street, it had bounced right through the big bay window of a house and finished up in their front room.

When the United manager got the news he rushed out and, discovering I was the culprit, gave me a lecture about bad ball control. From 6ft tall, I felt just 2ft high.

So my dreams of playing for United had well and truly gone out through the window, a case of over and out.

MR L BRIDDON (SHEFFIELD)

IN A MUDDLE

MY SON (aged 10) was doing a kid's crossword and was having trouble finishing it. So he asked me to check his answers so far. I soon discovered his mistake: one of the clues read "Seaman (6)" and instead of writing the correct answer ("Sailor"), he'd written "goalie"!

MRS A MULLER (HEDNESFORD)

And I bet you a tenner Andy Cole still won't score.

PANE IN THE GLASS

WHEN JÜRGEN Klinsmann moved into a flat in Hampstead he was surprised to hear a tapping on his window one morning before he roused himself for training. You see, the flat in question wasn't on ground level! He discovered the creator of the noise was a window cleaner, also a keen Tottenham supporter, who wanted to make the acquaintance of the latest high-price arrival at White Hart Lane.

Klinsmann reacted with typical continental charm, inviting the willing wiper and his offspring to watch him train. So when, after his decision to return to Germany, his former chairman Alan Sugar said he wouldn't use Klinsmann's shirt to wash his car, perhaps he should have considered giving it to the window cleaner. It's unlikely he'd have taken the same view...

WOULD SEAMAN HAVE SAVED IT?

WHEN NICK HORNBY wrote *Fever Pitch*, the diary of an Arsenal supporter, he couldn't have realised it would become not only a best-seller but a film. For the latter, former Gunners keeper John Lukic (who rejoined the club as cover for David Seaman, the man who replaced him, in 1996) was employed to star in a 'replay' of the 1989 season when his failure to stop a Dean Saunders penalty made the title race go down to the last game at Liverpool, which Arsenal eventually won 2-0.

Filmed at Fulham's Craven Cottage (deputising for the now all-seater Highbury), Lukic had to shoot the scene several times, occasionally 'saving' by accident in an attempt to look as if he tried. Then, after successfully being beaten, he had to endure good-natured chants of "Seaman would have saved it!" about his successor.

CLOUGHIE'S CONGRATS

BRIAN CLOUGH WAS apparently a big fan of Ruud Gullit. So when the Chelsea and Holland midfielder was chosen to succeed Glenn Hoddle as manager of the Stamford Bridge side after Hoddle took the England job, Cloughie was keen to add his congratulations. Having obtained Chelsea's ground number from directory enquiries, he finally managed to raise the switchboard. "Oh yes," he intoned in that familiar deadpan, "Is that Stamford Bridge? Put me through to that Ruud fella, will you?" Something must have gone wrong at the switchboard — for within seconds, he found himself talking to chairman Ken Bates!

LEAGUE OF NATIONS

THE FIGHT TO put soccer on the map in North America began long before the 1994 World Cup. Yet the North American Soccer League ran into problems by relying too heavily on outsiders. Some were famous, like Pelé and Franz Beckenbauer, but spare a thought for the coach of Dallas Tornado. His pre-match talks must have been worth listening to, because his side of 1968 contained players from Holland, England and Scandinavia — but not one American!

Dallas went on a world tour of 45 games before playing their first NASL fixture that season. On many occasions the host clubs were raising the American flag to salute players who, in some cases, had yet to set foot in the States at all...

Lift the other arm, Les, I still can't see it.

IT'S A VAIN GAME

IT'S COMMONLY thought that clubs in today's game change their strips regularly in order to generate more cash from merchandising — but Bolton Wanderers prove that this has been going on since the game began.

The Trotters began the 1881 season in a red strip, then changed to red and white quarters half-way through. Unhappy with this, they took to the field in 1884 with a tasteful salmon pink jersey before changing in mid-season to a white shirt with red spots! They then experimented with 'lily' shirts and blue and white before finally opting for the familiar white shirt and blue shorts that they sport today. It just goes to show that even football clubs have been fashion victims in their younger days!

THREE SINGING LIONS

FOOTBALLERS SHOULD always be discouraged from singing — but those who have managed to find success include Peter Osgood ('Chirpy Chirpy Cheep Cheep'), Jeff Astle ('Sweet Water'), Kevin Keegan ('Head Over Heels') and Chris Waddle and Glenn Hoddle ('Diamond Lights').

There have, however, been more tuneful efforts. Elton John's recruited the Watford first-team squad to back him on record, while Liverpool's Craig Johnston wrote his side's 1988 hit 'The Anfield Rap' which made the Top 3 — arguably through musical merit.

Would you mind awfully popping over to the seating area, there's a good chap.

CROWD(ED) HOUSE

FANATICAL FOLLOWING

A FEW YEARS AGO at a Peterborough v Cardiff match, Paul Culpin was attacking for the home side when about 30 Cardiff fans invaded the pitch and chased Paul down the wing. Paul looked over his shoulder, took three more paces, shot from 25 metres and scored.

The Cardiff fans turned and trudged back to the rest of their dejected mates.

D COTTERILL (WITTERING)

WAKE UP

IN OCTOBER 1954, when Crystal Palace drew 1-1 with Reading at Selhurst Park, one bored home supporter yawned so wide on his way out that he had to be taken to hospital and treated for lockjaw!

MR A EDMANS (READING)

PLENTY OF ROOM

MEMBERS OF THE Falkirk sporting fraternity who thought they had better set off early for the vital Scottish Second Division basement battle between East Stirlingshire and Leigh on 15 April 1939, need not have bothered. For only 32 spectators turned up — the lowest attendance for a senior League game in Britain. There were no reports of any crowd disturbances.

MR C PEARSON (COALVILLE)

MESSING ABOUT ON THE RIVER

UNTIL THEY BUILT the Eric Miller Stand, Fulham Football Club's long-suffering supporters could not only swop ends during a match by walking along the Riverside terrace. They were also able to watch the boat race on a certain Saturday in the spring, turning as one to regard the action on the water (which was inevitably more dramatic than that on the pitch), while those males caught short at half-time were often seen to do the unmentionable, augmenting the Thames in a spectacular – if insanitary – arc!

LOSERS' FINAL NO LOSS

WE OFTEN HEAR people in the game complain of fixture congestion, yet the five seasons at the start of the 1970s saw one of the least attractive matches ever take its place in the English footballing calendar. It was a play-off for third and fourth place between the losing FA Cup semi-finalists. They say it's worse to lose in the semis than have a day out at Wembley... and the poor crowds that greeted these games suggested fans, like players, would prefer to nurse their hangovers in private.

The first game in 1970 attracted 15,000, probably because Manchester United were involved. They beat Watford 2-0, but by the 1974 clash between Leicester and Burnley, only 4,000 could be persuaded to show up to see the Turf Moor side triumph by a single goal. The fixture was thenceforth scrapped... and few have missed it.

LONG WAY FROM LISBON

CELTIC WERE THE first British side to claim club football's greatest prize, the European Cup. Their 2-1 win against Inter Milan in Lisbon in 1967 has gone down in history, and rightly so. Although the behaviour of their fans was exemplary when compared to Rangers' followers four years later in Rotterdam, there are tales of a number of Celts who missed the game. Legend has it they were last seen boarding a plane at Glasgow Airport – for Milan...

MISTAKEN IDENTITY

RANMERE FANS resent being lumped in with fans of their local rivals Liverpool
nd Everton. As anyone who's visited their Prenton Park ground will know,
ey're separated from their neighbours by the width of the River Mersey, and
sing the following: "Do not be mistaken, do not be misled/We're not
ousers, we're from Birkenhead/You can keep your Cathedral, and your Pier
ead/We're not Scousers, we're from Birkenhead!"

YOU'RE TOO OLD(HAM) FOR THAT

OLDHAM MADE THEIR debut in the First Division in 1910. Despite
the larger crowds that turned up to watch top-class opposition
playing at Boundary Park, it was noted that the gate receipts had
not increased — in fact, they had fallen rapidly.

On investigation, the board observed that many young men were
paying half-price at the turnstiles by claiming to be at school. To
remedy this, the club posted notices at the next home game. They
read: 'Boys enter here. Admission 3d.' and 'Boys with whiskers —
Two turnstiles up. Admission 6d.' The gate receipts went up... and
the team stayed up!

PARDON GRANTED

CELEBRITY FANS ARE always good for a club — like Robbie Williams, the ex-
Take That singer, who added several noughts to replica shirt sales at Port
Vale when he wore his on stage, giving his favourite club a kick in the
coffers, so to speak. Hugh Grant, a season ticket holder at Craven Cottage
with girlfriend Liz Hurley, hasn't yet proved as profitable for the club he
supports. On the other hand, it's given the perennial chant "You're going
down with the Fulham" a whole new dimension...

JAIL FAILURE

ENGLAND'S PROGRESS IN Euro '96 captured the attention of millions
nationwide — yet those who were quite literally captured were unable to
see the tournament through. Prisoners at Parkhurst Jail on the Isle of
Wight were allowed to watch the first half of England's semi-final with
Germany, but were then scheduled to return to their cells and so missed
the nail-biting penalty shootout.

The staff, who at least video-recorded the remainder of the match, had
promised to waive their tea-time had England got to the Final to avoid a
repetition. "They're usually locked up at that time of the afternoon,"
explained an official, before adding: "the inmates, not the staff..."

THE MAN IN BLACK

'ER INDOORS

NOTHING WAS GOING right for me during one particular game, so I was taking out my frustrations on the ref by constantly moaning at him. After one moan too many, the man in black stopped the game, called me over and said: "For Christ's sake wee man, the only reason I come out of the house on a Saturday is to get away from somebody like you... Now shut it!"

MR J BOAG (GREENOCK)

BAD TIMING

A PLAYER WAS summoned to the referee after commiting a rather nasty tackle. He was told that he was getting booked and asked the ref what for.

"You are being cautioned for a late challenge," said the ref. "But I got there as quick as I could!" was the reply.

MR R McLAUCHLAN (PAISLEY)

WOMEN AND CHILDREN FIRST

BEFORE A GAME STARTED one day, it was in doubt due to heavy rain. The ref said: "Any more rain during the game and I may have to abandon the match." So the game started and half-way through the second half — with the pitch like a bog — down came the rain, turning it into a swimming pool. I looked at the ref, after falling into a pool of muck and water, and said: "I think you should abandon the game now, sir." The ref stared at me and grinned, saying "Come on man, I've been refereeing football matches for 15 years and I've yet to see a football player drown. Get on with it!"

MR J BOAG (GREENOCK)

Hey, Giancarlo. I know italian referees are corrupt, but I'd prefer money.

ARE YOU BLIND, REF?!

THE REFEREE IS blessed (or cursed?) with the task of laying down the letter of the law and making sure that the game runs smoothly, as well as dealing with several thousand fans who inevitably think that they can do a better job.

In the light of this, it's hardly surprising that a referee makes the occasional mistake. After all, they're only human. But eyebrows were raised when wayward decisions become the rule rather than the exception – and that was the case with referee Keith Butcher.

Before kick-off in a match, a linesman had to point out that both teams were wearing the same colour kits. More than once he awarded a penalty when it was blatantly obvious that the decision should have been a free-kick to the defending side. He even admitted he couldn't tell the difference between his yellow and red cards.

It turned out that Mr Butcher had managed to become a fully qualified referee despite the fact he was colour blind!

1-0 TO THE REF

A BARROW SHOT going harmlessly wide struck referee Ian Robinson and deflected into the net for the only goal of the 1968 clash with Plymouth. In an interview afterwards, one Plymouth player said: "It was a long way to go to be beaten by a goal from the ref."

MR C PEARSON (COALVILLE)

THE PROFESSIONALS

WHAT CAR?

WHILE WATCHING MY local side, St Mirren, in a Premier League fixture some years ago, a friend made comment on young Scotland international full-back Maurice Malpas.

He said of the Dundee United starlet, "I think that Maurice Malpas is great" to which another replied, "Aye, but the Minor was better and you could get a better deal on insurance."

MR R McLAUCHLAN (PAISLEY)

THE SCOT FROM RIO

IN THE EARLY Eighties (1981-82 to be precise), when Ipswich were a bit of a force they entertained Southampton at Portman Road in a high scoring League game 5-3 in Ipswich's favour. All Ipswich's five goals came from Alan Brazil.

An after-match comment by Southampton's Yugoslavian goalkeeper Iva Katalinic, whose team had incidently been top of the First Division at the time was, "I wish that man would go back to Brazil."

MR A BRIDGES (STEVENSTON

But I am calm, ref!

OVER HERE, DAD!

THERE ARE MANY famous fathers and sons in football — but few who've shared a pitch. The exceptions to bridge the generation gap were the Herds, Alec and David. Alec's finest hours had been spent in the service of Manchester City, and he was in the twilight of his career at neighbouring Stockport when son David started coming through the junior ranks. After several early-1950s games alongside Dad, the young lad would go on to Arsenal before making his own mark on Manchester football — in the colours of United.

250 Grand and only Venables and Graham Taylor to beat? Yeah, I'll take it.

FOR HE'S A JOLLY GOOD FELLOW

HIS OWN GOAL having secured promotion for Nottingham Forest in 1977, grateful Forest supporters voted Millwall's Jon Moore their Player of the Year that evening.

MR C PEARSON (COALVILLE)

SMALL, BUT PERFECTLY FORMED

THERE WERE MANY people who doubted whether Brazilian star Juninho would make it in the English game because of his small stature, and some would say that he has still to prove himself.

However, the Brazilian striker is not the smallest player to have played in the Football League. The lightest player on record is W Hepworth, who played for Barnsley in the 1890s. He tipped the scales at a staggering seven stone five pounds.

YOU ARE WHAT YOU EAT

THE IMPORTANCE OF diet in footballers' lifestyles is now under the microscope, with the traditional pre-match steak and chips giving way to high-carbohydrate pasta and other foods designed to help give players energy during the all-important 90 minutes.

Two exceptions to the rule are Leeds United's Tony Yeboah and former Elland Road stalwart Gordon Strachan, now player/assistant manager at Coventry City. Yeboah credited his great start in English football to a diet of Yorkshire Pudding, a delicacy he'd never encountered before on his footballing travels in Africa and the Continent. Strachan, by contrast, thrives on a supplement of...seaweed tablets! "I don't know what it does for my performance on the pitch," he jokes, "but it's done wonders for my swimming!"

DING! DING!

FOOTBALLERS AT ALL levels have always had their differences — but it's rare for team-mates to come to blows! Those who did include Derek Hales and Mike Flanagan of Charlton, and Graeme Le Saux and David Batty of Blackburn, the latter during a European Cup game away to Spartak Moscow.

OFF

LUCKY BREAK?

WHEN FULL-BACK David Whelan broke his leg while playing for Blackburn against Wolves in the 1960 FA Cup Final, it effectively ended his career. What was also immediately apparent was the fact that his team's chances left the pitch with him. Norman Deeley, the player he was marking, put the game beyond Rovers' reach by scoring twice in the second half. Whelan quit football after a short comeback spell with Crewe to go into retailing and, having made his first million, went into sports goods. Had his football career continued as planned, who knows if he would have followed that ultra-successful path? He later re-entered football when he became chairman of Wigan Athletic in the 1990s.

I can't sing either.

UNLUCKY FOR SOME

STEVE MILTON, making his debut in goal for Halifax Town in 1934, let in 13 goals at Stockport in Division Three North on 6 January. Town lost 13-0.

MR C PEARSON (COALVILLE)

THE DROUGHT OF '93

IN EARLY 1993 Third Division Hartlepool, bored with mid-table anonymity, gallantly set about shattering the endurance record for the longest spell without a goal. Following Andy Saville's last-minute penalty in the 1-0 FA Cup giant-killing defeat of Crystal Palace, they contrived to go over 13 matches without hitting the back of the net. The total stood at an impressive 1,22 minutes when on 6 March at Blackpool, Saville had the misfortune to score the equalizer in a 1-1 draw. His punishment was immediate: a transfer to Birmingham City.

MR C PEARSON (COALVILLE)

CLOUGHIE'S CLANGER

BRIAN CLOUGH DIDN'T make too many mistakes in his managerial career, but when he made them they could be big ones. Selling star striker Teddy Sheringham and buying Justin Fashanu — not at the same time — probably top the list at Nottingham Forest. Neither was as embarrassing as when he paraded winger Ian Storey-Moore around the Baseball Ground when manager of Derby.

Clough was convinced he'd got his man, but Storey-Moore's wife had other ideas and the player — ironically a Nottingham Forest player — eventually put pen to paper for Manchester United.

SEEING RED

IT MAY NOT be all that well known, but George Best is one of the first ever players to receive a red card.

The red and yellow card system was introduced on Saturday 2 October 1976. On that day the bold George was playing for Fulham against Southampton at the Dell when he was given his marching orders for foul and abusive language.

MR A BRIDGES (STEVENSTON)

A FRUITY PROBLEM

THE BIGGEST TALKING point of the 1995-96 season for Nottingham Forest fans was Jason Lee's hairstyle of tied-back dreadlocks. Its similarity to a pineapple was first pointed out in public by the *Fantasy Football* TV team of Skinner and Baddiel, which led to visiting fans singing 'He's got a pineapple on his head' to the tune of the spiritual 'He's got the whole world in his hands.'

The striker's form suffered, leading to manager Frank Clark allegedly complaining about the two 'middle class wide-boys' who'd blighted his striker's career. Lee, transfer-listed in the 1996 close season, took matters into his own hands in July by shaving off his hair completely.

TEL'S FEATHERED FRIEND

EVERTON WING-HALF Terry Darracott was an industrious 1970s performer, but not a player noted for his speed. Before one particular game, he caught sight of a pigeon with an injured wing which had somehow got onto the pitch but was unable to fly away when the players made their entrance. Keen to do the right thing, he picked up the bird in both hands and gently took it to the sidelines for someone to look after. As he did so, a cry came up from one of the fans. "Bloody 'ell, that Terry Darracott's getting quick — he's catching flippin' racing pigeons now!"

POOLS ARE FOOLS

MANY A FOOTBALL League side has come to grief against non-League opposition in that leveller we call the FA Cup, but few over the years have come a cropper quite as often as Hartlepool United. From the 1925-26 season to 1929-30, they exited four times in those five seasons to sides from the semi-pro game.

North-Eastern League outfits Blyth Spartans and Carlisle beat them before Halifax, like Hartlepool in the Third Division North, took a turn in 1927-28. Next came another North-Eastern League side Spennymoor before Midland League Scunthorpe concluded a unique half-decade of humiliation.

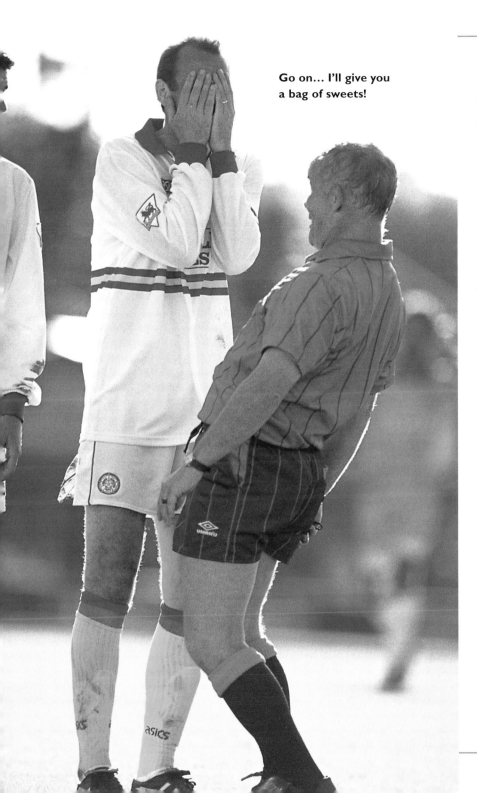

**Go on… I'll give you
a bag of sweets!**

GONG WITH THE WIND

THE SCOTTISH CUP Final in 1977 had a bizarre postscript when, after stopping to talk to some disabled kids, Celtic skipper Kenny Dalglish lost his medal. Having had it jolted out of his hand by a wellwisher, he, Celtic's trainer and team-mate Peter Latchford, searched desperately to retrieve it, even tearing apart advertising hoardings on the off-chance it had fallen in one.

The police eventually persuaded a tearful Dalglish to continue his lap of honour and leave it to them to find it. They did — it had fallen into the umbrella of one of the wheelchair-bound fans!

A SECOND CHANCE

EXETER CITY MANAGER Brian Godfrey was so appalled by his team's 5-1 defeat against Millwall in 1982 that as punishment he made his team play Millwall's reserves the next day. He was even more astonished to see his team lose 1-0 to the Lions' second team.

MR C PEARSON (COALVILLE)

THE GREATEST
— FINNEY OR MATTHEWS?

1948, ENGLAND VERSUS Portugal: Stanley Matthews centred and Mortensen dived in to head a goal. He jumped up, ran back with arms raised and celebrated with Matthews.

Near half-time, Finney went down the left wing, beat two men and put over a great cross. Mortensen hardly had to move to head it into the net, but he immediately held his head and almost fell to the ground. Early in the second half, Finney again made a brilliant run and put over another superb centre which was again headed home by Mortensen. Once more, he held his head in his hands.

With ten minutes left, it was Matthews' turn to beat his marker and send over a beautiful cross. Again Mortensen leapt and sent a bullet header into the top corner.

He jumped for joy and ran the length of the pitch in celebration. At full time, as the players left the pitch, Finney spoke to Mortensen. "Stan," he said, "how is it when I cross the ball you head it and act as though you're about to collapse head in hands, but when Matthews crosses you run round the pitch overjoyed?"

"No offence, Tom," replied Mortensen, "it's just that playing with Stan at Blackpool he knows to point the lace towards the goal."

MR R GIDDINS (ROCHDALE)

If we were birds we'd get 800 quid a night for this.

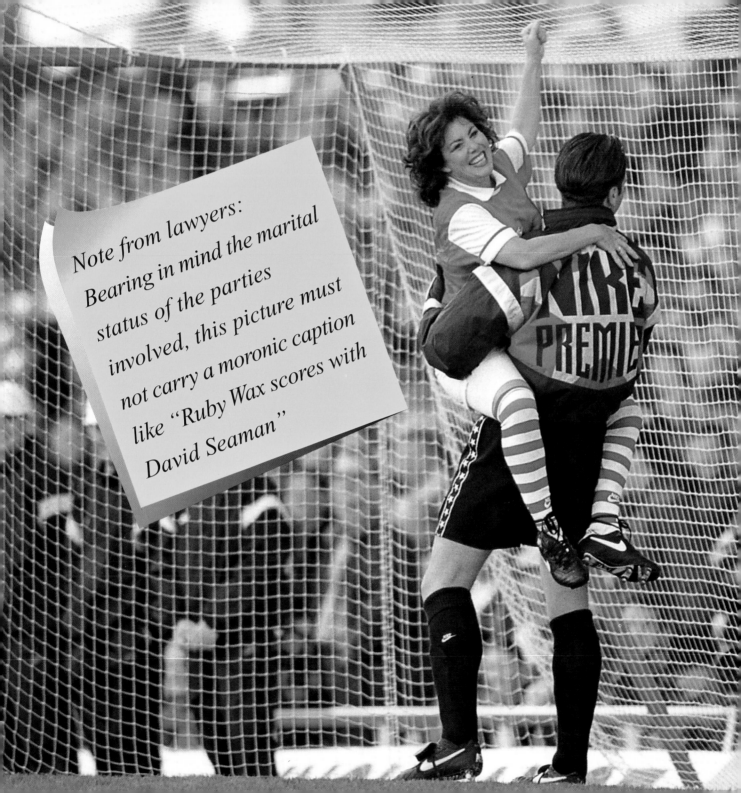

Note from lawyers: Bearing in mind the marital status of the parties involved, this picture must not carry a moronic caption like "Ruby Wax scores with David Seaman"

BOSS ON THE ROCKS

THE LATE, GREAT Manchester United supremo Matt Busby found himself near a football ground and, on the off-chance, decided to drop in and pay his respects to the manager, an old friend. He found the boss sitting at his desk with a glass in one hand and a half-empty bottle of Scotch in the other.

"I didn't know you took a drink," exclaimed Busby in surprise. "Not before I had this job," came the answer. "But I was warned that being a football manager would either drive me mad or drive me to drink — and I'm damned sure it won't drive me mad!"

NODDING ACQUAINTANCES

EVERTON CENTRE-FORWARD Dixie Dean and Liverpool goalkeeper Elisha Scott were the keenest of rivals on the pitch, facing each other a number of times in crucial derbies. So intense was their determination to get one over on the other that, when they once met in the street, Dean nodded in friendly recognition to his opponent... and was startled to see Scott throw himself full-length into the gutter to make the "save"!

SEAN AND HEARD

HE MAY HAVE been a motivational and tactical genius as a manager, but England's World Cup-winning boss Alf Ramsey was not one for social events. Yet as the country rolled out the red carpet for the national team, he was obliged to do the done thing and offer up votes of thanks to those who played host to the sporting heroes. On one occasion, the England squad were invited on the set of the latest James Bond film to meet the stars, and later a nervous Ramsey stepped up to the rostrum as they were about to depart. "I'm sure the players would like to join me in thanking Seen (sic) Connery for his hospitality," is how it reportedly came out!

AND ON THE SEVENTH DAY...

ONE IN THE OVEN

I WAS GETTING cleaned up after a football match in the morning when someone shouted "What's that burning in the oven?"

I rushed to open the oven door as I knew what was burning — and lo and behold there it was, dark brown, burnt on the bottom. The crackling round the edges was done to a turn. No, it was not a piece of roast pork for dinner but my leather football boots, cooked beyond repair.

Having played one game in the morning we were due to play another in the afternoon but my boots were sodden wet and heavy. Drying them in front of the fire was too slow, so I put them in the oven but someone must have closed the door.

I've heard of people 'cooking the books' but the last person I can remember cooking the boots was Charlie Chaplin in the film *The Gold Rush* — so I was in good company.

MR L BRIDDON (SHEFFIELD)

THE MAGIC SPONGE

DURING A VERY intense Sunday morning Cup game, there was about 30-40 of us watching our mates play when near the end of the game a heavy tackle went in on one of their players.

They immediately called for the 'magic' bucket and sponge. The opposition, being away from home, only had a couple of subs, a manager and one poor supporter to cheer them on. This supporter remonstrated from the touchline and his team-mates on the pitch were shouting at him to bring on the bloody bucket.

He did. He carried out the bucket and sponge, all the way to the centre circle and it was then everyone realised what he was saying. It had no water in it! But he still carried it out... The whole place erupted with laughter and the player got up off the floor.

MR T ELMER (CHESSINGTON)

30

"Ian's the dark horse of the England camp," naaahah!

MOONLIGHTING

CHARLIE WILLIAMS played 158 games as a defender for Doncaster Rovers — but his performances as a singer on the coach to and from games won him just as much recognition from his team-mates as performances on the pitch. His games on Saturday afternoons became double-headers with club appearances in the evenings, mixing humour with some Nat King Cole impressions — and when the TV series *The Comedians* came along his new career was off and running.

A Tough Break

The following incident happened at a local senior night match. The pitch was muddy and it was pouring with rain.

A player went in for a tackle and got caught on his ankle. The ref stopped play and signalled to the physio to attend the player who was on the far side of the pitch.

The physio was rather a large chap about 18 stone, he ran as fast as he could to the other side of the pitch to attend to the player. Not realising his lightning speed, he tried to stop, sliding on his backside and landing full force onto the player's good leg, fracturing his fibula in two places. On getting to his feet he asked the player, "Where does it hurt?"!

NJ Bullimore (Peterborough)

Instant Promotion

Celtic's 1960s legend John Hughes had just recovered from injury and was leaving the training ground when a reporter asked him if he'd be playing on Saturday. "Oh yes, I'll be ready," came the reply. The next day's paper duly carried the story that he would be in the team. That morning, manager Jock Stein invited Hughes into his office and told him to sit in his chair. Handing the bemused winger a pen and paper, he said: "I see you're playing on Saturday. So you may as well write down the rest of the team while you're at it."

A Pitch Too Far

Robert Andrews (name changed to prevent a libel suit) manages or should I say mis-manages, AFC Oldpike, for whom I have played for ten years.

Five years ago, during one of our wettest Novembers on record, we had an important relegation battle and Robert (nicknamed Hagar the Horrible) decided that the match should be played at all cost. It was an away game and unbeknown to our opposition, he went down to their pitch on the Saturday and spent three hours with a hand-held pitch fork, clearing the ground and removing the water. He excitedly phoned me at tea time to tell me what he had done and that match would definitely be played.

We travelled to their pitch the next day, only to be met by the referee who called the match off due to a waterlogged pitch. Hagar stormed past the ref and was astonished to find two teams playing on the pitch he had prepared the previous day.

"Why are they playing on your pitch?" screamed Hagar.

"That's not ours," replied the opposing manager. "We moved onto the other one last year."

Needless to say this was like a lake and fit only for ducks!

Mr D Teall (Hull)

Confused!

A match involving Partick Thistle saw the Jags use both their permitted subs, only to see one of their players go down injured midway through the second half.

The physio ran on to treat the player and the manager John Lambie looked on anxiously as the physio informed him that the player was concussed and did not know who he was.

"Great, tell him he's Pelé and there's twenty minutes left!" was the sympathetic reply.

Mr R McLauchlan (Paisley)

And it's even better when my friend does it.

SINK YER TEETH IN!

IRISHMAN TOMMY Godwin, who played for Leicester before recording 350 League games for Bournemouth, was one of the game's great characters. After he retired in 1961 he was asked if he had any regrets about his career. He answered that if he could have his time again he'd have worn his false teeth for one of his 13 Eire appearances instead of leaving them in his dressing room as was his habit. The Republic were 2-0 up against Denmark with ten minutes to go and the opposition fans, unhappy with his supposed time-wasting, decided to pelt his goal with apples!

MAN-TO MAN MARKING

I WAS MANAGER of Seafar Villa Boys U-14s Club when we went to play a Cup tie in Glasgow. We were winning quite easily when I decided to make a substitution. I got the ref's attention and shouted for my player to come off and to my amazement one of the opposing players came off with him. When I asked this player what he was doing, he said to me his manager told him to follow my player everywhere as he was our best player. It was then the opposing manager shouted over to him to get back on the park, but the lad told him he had no one to mark and walked into the dressing room amid a lot of laughter and applause.

I still laugh to this day about that incident, and I've been involved in football for 30 years as a manager and player.

F DAVIDSON (CUMBERNAULD)

BOOTS AND SLIPPERS

UNORTHODOX TRAINING methods often played a part in shaping the great players of the past. The wearing of a carpet slipper on his good foot during informal matches to encourage him to use his weaker one made Bobby Charlton a two-footed player to be feared. Over at Chester, centre-forward Ron Davies developed a fearsome aerial ability when his manager suggested he tried playing in army boots: once relieved of these clod-hoppers, the jumping power he exhibited not only made him his club's top scorer but brought Welsh international honours and a series of big-money moves that ended up at Old Trafford... just as Bobby Charlton retired!

A PLAY-ANYWHERE PERFORMER

UTILITY MEN MAY be out of fashion in today's specialist game, bu football once thrived on them – players who'd turn out wherever th boss wanted. Take John Hewie, a one-club man who served Charlto with distinction between 1951 and 1965. He played for the Addicks i every position, including four games in goal. His versatility won him Scottish caps, but he also managed to play against them for Sout Africa in 1956... and, to complicate matters still further, this all-roun sportsman played international baseball... for England!

You want to slow down a bit, you're working up a right sweat.

SAM THE MAN

IN APRIL 1924 Sam Chedgzoy scored from a corner in a match involving Everton and Tottenham Hotspur – which although not a common occurrence, is not unheard of. But this particular goal sealed a place for Chedgzoy in the record books.

After studying the rules of the game in some detail, Sam was confident that he had found a loophole and bet that he could dribble the ball from the corner and score. This he did, to the surprise of a confused Spurs defence – and, although the goal was initially ruled out, it was eventually allowed to stand as no rules had been broken. This prompted a change in the rules, but not before Sam won his bet... and Everton the game 5-2!

BOXING CLEVER WITH SHANKS

ILL SHANKLY'S TEAM talks were the stuff of legend, as Tom Saunders, a oot-room regular during his reign, recalls.

"The players waited for their instructions and Shankly began to peak and continued for some 15 minutes. Not about the opposition, or ven football. Oh, no! Boxing was the sole subject for a quarter of an our. He then switched to football but quickly brought proceedings to halt. 'Don't let's waste time! This bloody lot can't play at all.' With hat, the team talk was rapidly brought to a close."

DOUBLE VISION

IT SEEMS THAT Oldham Athletic like to keep business in the family as it were — for not only have they had five sets of brothers playing at the club, they have also had six father and son combinations during their history.

The most effective combination must surely have been twins Paul and Ron Futcher, who played for the Latics in the 1980s. Paul was rated as one of the best defenders in the Second Division, while brother Ron averaged a goal every other game during his time at the club. It's not surprising, really. The opposition defence probably thought they were seeing double!

Bloody 'ell Stan, the boss'll want more than Mr Ed impressions for eight bloody million.

THE BEST REVENGE

WHEN THE FA BANNED Manchester United's wing wizard George Best for six weeks, the Northern Ireland ace had plenty of time to plan his revenge. The unfortunate team to suffer was Northampton Town, facing United in the FA Cup Fifth Round. The lowly Cobblers suffered as Best went through his repertoire, scoring six in an 8-2 win.

Best later admitted he "wanted to show everybody. But after about 70 minutes, when I'd scored six, I didn't want to score any more. So I spent the last 20 minutes of the game at left-back." Northampton keeper Kim Book's son once called up a radio phone-in when Best was recalling the event to insist that his Dad actually made a save in the game... but Best, somewhat unsportingly, denied it!

SCHEMING SHANKS

A PRANK OF Bill Shankly in the early 1960s at fortress Anfield was to have one of the back room staff (ie Bootroom Team) at the time, be it Rueben Bennet, Bob Paisley, Ronnie Moran or Joe Fagan, wait till the opposition was arriving at Anfield and going into their dressing room, then pop out with a large box of toilet rolls. "Could you take these in with you, lads, and put them in the toilet for me?" The opposition's faces were nearly always a picture, and the Liverpool lads would be rolling about the dressing room in fits of laughter, easing any pre-match tension in the home dressing room.

MR A BRIDGES (STEVENSTON)

The Bosman Agreement altered the face of football, making players open to all kinds of offers.

It's no use **Gazza**, Sheryl will guess you're here.

SPOT THE MISTAKE!

NO-ONE HAD ever failed to convert a penalty in an FA Cup Final until the unfortunate John Aldridge of Liverpool had his kick saved by Wimbledon captain Dave Beasant in 1988. Not only did this ensure that Lawrie Sanchez's first-half goal proved decisive, but also meant that the mighty Reds, who ran away with the League Championship, missed out on their second Double of the decade. It couldn't have happened to a nicer bloke — and, whether or not it had anything to do with the miss, he left Liverpool on the return of Ian Rush, the man he'd replaced, from Juventus.

HE DIVED, HONEST!

THE PENALTY KICK has become part and parcel of the modern game, and it's destroyed the dreams of more than one supporter. One only has to look to the agonising defeat of England by Germany in the semi-finals of both Euro '96 and World Cup '90 in penalty shootouts to see the power of the spot-kick.

Penalties were introduced in 1891, despite protests from many players who considered them a slur on their sportsmanship. The first was scored by John Heath of Wolverhampton against Accrington on 14 September 1891.

Since this time the spot-kick has become a specialty and most teams have a penalty taker like Peter Noble of Burnley — who didn't miss one of his 27 penalties between 1974-79. There are also goalkeepers who specialise in stopping penalties, notably Fred Mearn of Kettering who saved 19 in the 1903-04 season.

LEFT, RIGHT AND CENTRE!

PRE-WAR CENTRE-FORWARD Ronnie Rooke was an imposing player, able to strike a penalty cleanly and powerfully with either foot. Furthermore, he claimed his slightly bandy-legged stance gave him the advantage of being able to keep a goalkeeper guessing not only where he intended placing the ball — but which foot he was going to use!

On one occasion, facing Frank Swift of Manchester City and England, he struck the ball past him only to have the kick ruled out for some reason. On retaking it, he struck it with the other foot to equal effect. As he ran back towards the centre circle, he remarked to the referee "If you'd wanted me to do it again, ref, I reckon I'd have headed the third one past him!"

COTTAGE CURSES

ULHAM'S JOHNNY HAYNES was a player who could make the ball do hat he wanted, but sometimes understandably became frustrated ith team-mates who showed themselves not to be on the same avelength as himself. On one occasion, he trapped the ball and slid an nch-perfect pass to left-winger and best mate Trevor 'Tosh' hamberlain. Unfortunately, Chamberlain failed to control it and eceived the sharp end of the Maestro's tongue.

he referee stopped play and booked the irate Haynes, only for Tosh to ave the last word. Lumbering back to the scene of the booking, he erated the ref. "But ref," he pleaded. "He can call me a stupid ****. I'm n his side – and I am a stupid ****!"

MUTCH ADO ABOUT A PEN

THE VERY FIRST Cup Final to be broadcast live on TV happened in 1938 – and was decided by a very late goal indeed. The last minute of extra time saw Preston advancing on their opponents' Huddersfield, and Terriers defender Alf Young made a rare miscalculation in hauling down Preston's George Mutch.

A penalty was the result – but when none of the North End side stepped up to take the kick that would decide the fate of the Cup, Mutch himself hauled himself off the turf to shoulder the responsibility. The shot blasted against the crossbar and bounced down past goalkeeper Hesford into the net as the final whistle blew. To this day, the ball bears a white scar from its contact with the newly-painted crossbar.

Whatever happened to Gareth Southgate after that penalty?

You're eating him.

You do it for the adulation really.

FINAL DECISIONS

CUP FINAL REPLAYS have rarely seen changes made — but eyebrows were raised when Manchester United manager Alex Ferguson replaced jittery goalkeeper Jim Leighton with on-loan Les Sealey before his team took on Crystal Palace in 1990. His selection paid off as United battled to a 1-0 victory. Twenty years earlier, Chelsea had made a positional rather than personnel switch, swopping central defender Ron Harris and full-back David Webb, who'd been run ragged by Leeds winger Eddie Gray. The two played outstandingly in their new positions, while Webb, freed of Gray's attentions, even managed to score a goal in the 2-1 win. This match, played at Old Trafford, was the only FA Cup Final to be replayed away from Wembley since that ground became the venue for the showcase fixture in 1923.

THE CUP THAT CHEERS

THE FA CUP played for today is in fact the fourth trophy to bear the name. The first, which might have been kept in perpetuity by Wanderers, who took it three years running but gave it back, was stolen in 1895, while its successor only lasted until 1920 because the design had been 'pirated'.

The next Cup served for 80 years until 1991, and was won by Bradford City — coincidentally, hailing from the city where it was made — at the first time of asking. The newest trophy, a replica of the time-worn third, was first played for in 1992 — but Liverpool's Phil Thompson, a former player then on the coaching staff, dropped the lid that year and it was apparently dented so badly it would no longer fit on!

CUP COMES IN COLOURS

NO-ONE EVER thought to put coloured ribbons on the FA Cup until 1901 when Tottenham Hotspur, then a non-League side, did so during their celebrations of a replay defeat of Sheffield United. It's become a custom since then, the ribbons of both sides being put on the Cup and the losers eventually removed. That's now a continuing habit... but Spurs' feat has never been emulated by another non-League side.

Do you want any chocolate sauce with your crushed nuts?

Two inches lower and you're off my lad.

WHEN ASKED IF HE HAD
ANY SPARE TICKETS FOR
WIMBLEDON'S NEXT
HOME GAME, WARREN
BARTON REPLIED:

❝ How many do you
want? Two? You can
have the whole row if
you like! ❞

OUT OF THE COUNTRY

THE ONLY TIME the FA Cup has left England was when Cardiff City beat Arsenal in 1927. Ironically, Gunners keeper Danny Lewis, who was blamed by some for the game's only goal, was Welsh! In 1952, winners Newcastle took the trophy on a tour of South Africa, but it returned safely. In 1986, Liverpool kept the Cup in the country but won it with a team that contained not one Englishman – in international terms, anyway. The only player to have represented England at any level, Craig Johnston, was born in South Africa, while English-born Mark Lawrenson had chosen to represent Eire through a parental qualification.

BILLY'S FOGGED OFF

IT WAS A GREAT day when non-League Weymouth, managed by sometime Leicester and Manchester United boss Frank O'Farrell, reached the Fourth Round of the FA Cup, but an injury crisis left them without a fit goalkeeper. O'Farrell managed to secure Hull City veteran Billy Bly, who had just retired at the ripe old age of 42. The game, at Preston North End's Deepdale ground, kicked off in foggy conditions which eventually got so bad that the referee was forced to call the players off and abandon it.

Some while later, the Weymouth dressing room realised they were one man short. On returning to the pitch, O'Farrell found Bly still doggedly defending his goal. "I just assumed we were putting Preston under pressure at the other end," he explained.

❛ I left Man United because of Tommy Docherty. If he says good morning to you, you'd better check the weather outside. ❜

GEORGE BEST

RIGHT GAME — WRONG VENUE!

AMERICA'S PRESTIGIOUS soccer final, the Soccer Bowl, took place as usual in 1981... but not in the United States! Chicago Sting and New York Cosmos headed north of the border to play in front of a 37,000 crowd at Toronto's National Stadium. Chicago won the day, sneaking by the all-star Cosmos 1-0 in a shoot-out. Most Canadians, though, remained unmoved — as one sceptic later commented, it was a bit like playing the FA Cup Final at Hampden Park and expecting the Scots to show up!

THE NEARLY MEN

WHAT HAVE George Best, Johnny Haynes, George Cohen, Nobby Stiles and Martin Peters in common? All internationals, each was to register distinguished careers for club and country, the latter three even winning the game's highest honour, the World Cup. Yet while they were to enjoy their finest hour at Wembley, neither that much-honoured trio, nor Best nor Haynes, ever appeared in a single FA Cup Final.

Honourable Platt, try putting chopsticks in mouth, not eye.

HI! HO!...BILLY!?

THE FA CUP FINAL of 1923 has become known as the White Horse Final thanks to the heroic actions of PC George Scorey and his horse, Billy. It was the first year that football's showpiece was held at the new Wembley stadium and curiosity and high expectation resulted in nearly a quarter of a million people swarming into the 127,000 capacity ground.

Before long, the crowd had spilt onto the pitch and there was a very real possibility of a disaster taking place. Cue the national anthem and the mounted police who, between them, brought the crowd under control and moved them back onto the terraces. Despite the efforts of many mounted policemen, Constable Scorey was singled out by the media as the hero as press photographs showed the lone white horse holding thousands of supporters at bay. It's reported that when the officer, who had little interest in football, was asked by his girlfriend how his day had been, he replied: "Just ordinary, lass."

The Final, between Bolton and West Ham, started 45 minutes late and finished 2-0 to the northern side.

A BIRD IN THE GOAL...

EXETER CITY, that footballing outpost in Devon, have been responsible for initiating some unusual traditions over the years. One of the most controversial involved a fan dressing up as an eight-foot turkey in the shirt of local rivals Plymouth Argyle, then running round the pitch chased by the club's commercial manager waving a blunderbuss – all this to the sound of simulated gunfire from the PA system! The Football League took a dim view of these proceedings, and from then on the giant bustard donned an Exeter shirt and was pressed into service as goalkeeper in half-time penalty shoot-outs.

GOOD BOY, GINGER!

NEARLY EVERY SEASON the fates and fortunes of clubs around the country are decided in the final matches of the fixture lists as relegation battles rage to the bitter end. It is a time for heroes and villains but there can't be many clubs who, like Torquay, owe their survival to a police dog called Ginger!

In the final day of the 1986-87 season, Torquay were facing automatic relegation to the GM Vauxhall Conference as they were 2-1 down against Crewe with just minutes remaining.

Torquay defender Jim McNichol went down injured and was waiting for treatment when Ginger came bounding onto the pitch and promptly bit the prone player. The match was stopped for five minutes while McNichol received treatment and this gave Torquay time to rally. With just seconds remaining in injury time they scored an equaliser. A draw was enough to keep Torquay up, shading Lincoln on goal difference. After the match Torquay chairman, Lew Pope, said: "I'm going to buy Ginger the biggest steak in Torquay."

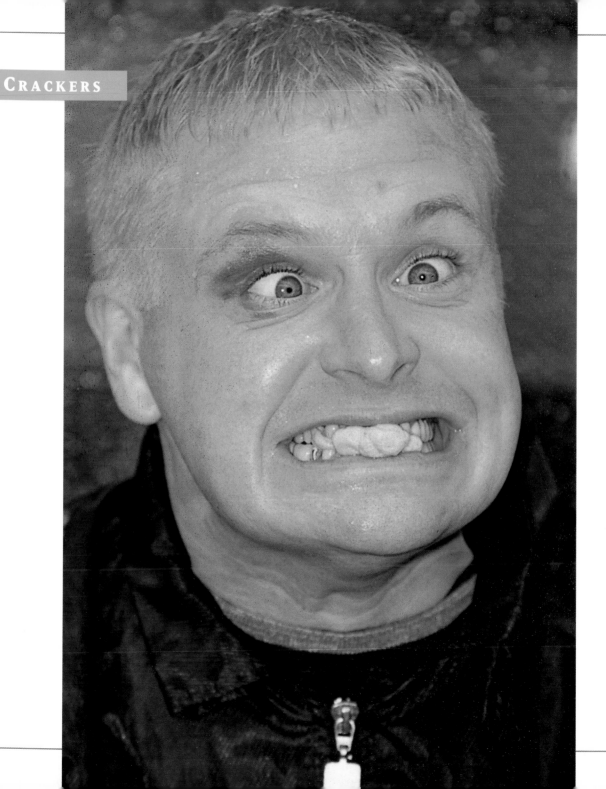

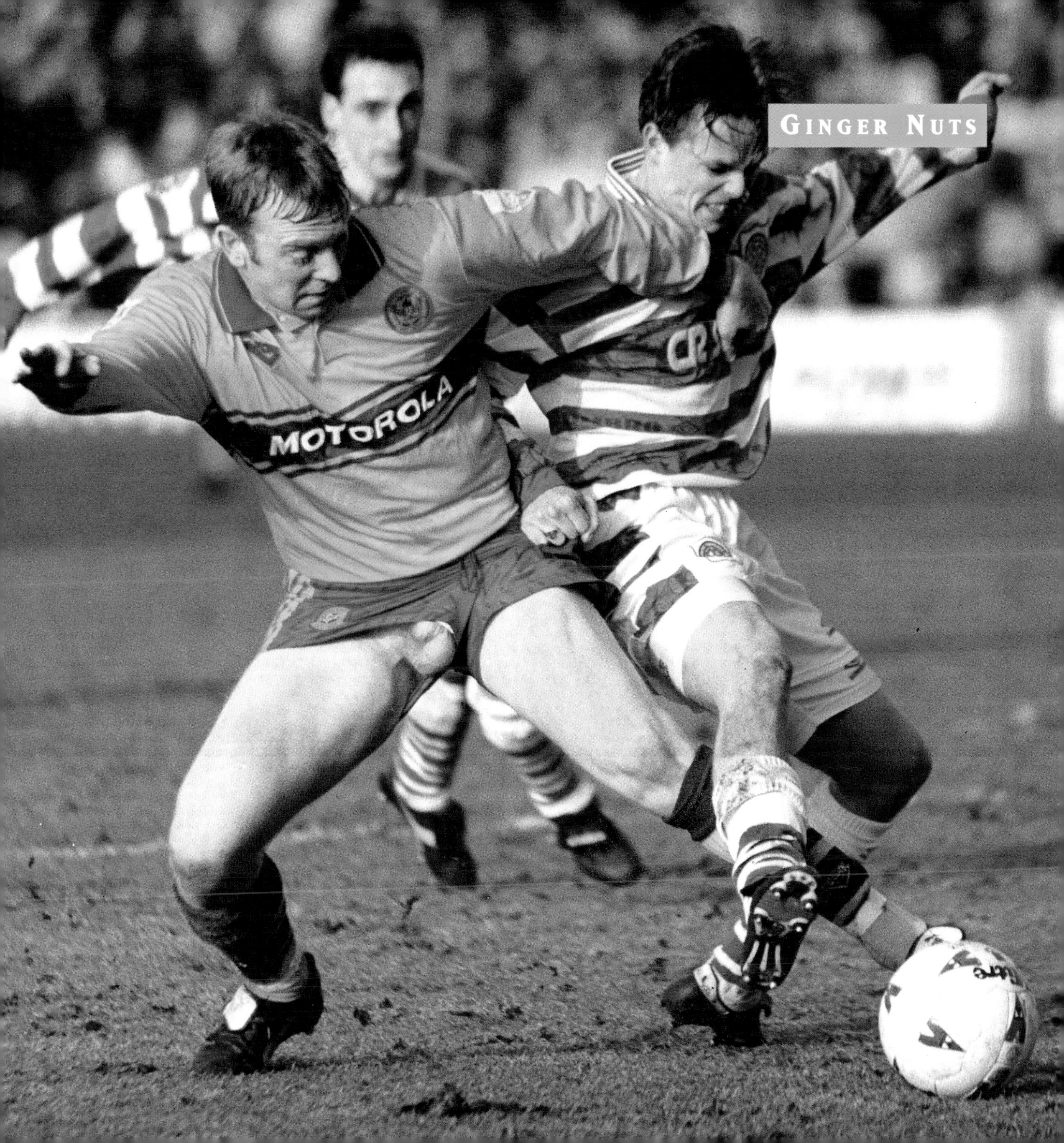
MOTOROLA

LISTEN LAD, FOOTBALL'S A GAME FOR HARD MEN

Let him know you're there.

Make him respect you.

Seize your moment...

...and we'll pull you off at half time!

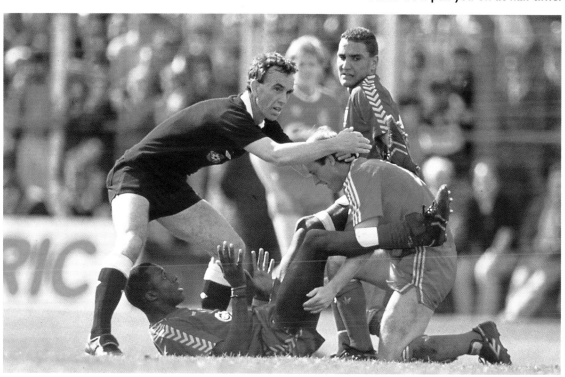

THE NUMBERS GAME

WHEN ALAN SHEARER signed for Newcastle United in July 1996 he insisted on the Number 9 shirt as part of the deal – so its previous occupant Les Ferdinand was delighted to hear manager Kevin Keegan explain that, though he'd be looking for another number, he wouldn't be looking for another club. The biggest disaster the Magpies faced apart from the interest on a £15 million bank loan was running out of the letter H after 2,000 replica shirts were sold in one day in the wake of the signing!

GEORGIE GOES GLASGOW

RANGERS AND CELTIC players aren't known for their togetherness – but they joined forces on one notable occasion to play a benefit match in aid of the Ibrox Disaster Fund after a tragedy in 1971 that led to 66 deaths. An Old Firm Select XI played a Scotland XI in front of a crowd of 81,405: George Best who, with Bobby Charlton and Peter Bonetti, became an honorary Glaswegian for the day, scored, but Scotland emerged 2-1 winners.

TWELVE AGAINST ELEVEN

WHEN FOOTBALL RESUMED after the war, Moscow Dynamo toured Britain in the autumn of 1945 and took part in some memorable matches. They drew with Chelsea, beat Cardiff and Arsenal (while complaining about the number of guests the Gunners fielded), then made their way north to face Rangers.

When the Glasgow club asked to play Jimmy Caskie, whose transfer from Hibs was in the process of going through, the Russians threatened to return south of the border, claiming he was another 'guest'. Rangers relented, and a thrilling 2-2 draw was the result. Unusually, though, Dynamo played five minutes of the second half with 12 men when a substitute came on but no-one went off... and the ref didn't notice!

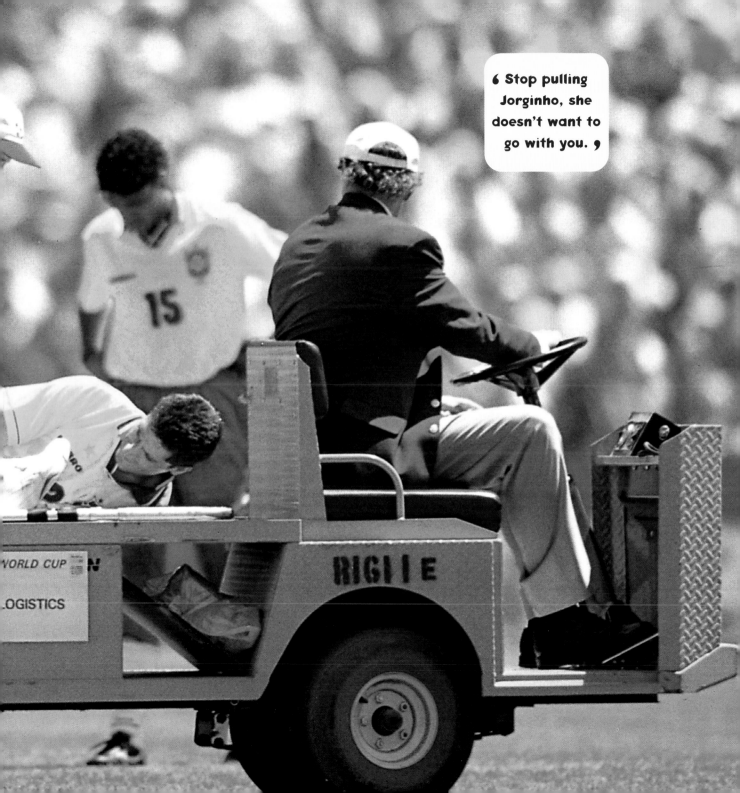

RED FACES FOR GREY SHIRTS

MANCHESTER UNITED have been leaders in the development of 'change strips' — kits of different colours to be used when teams' shirts clash. They had been criticised for the number of these devised, the argument being that they were attempting to maximise souvenir sales. Yet after successful trials of green and yellow, blue and white and — most strikingly — all black, the Old Trafford team fell foul of their fourth choice, grey. They went in 3-0 down at half-time in their 1996 clash with Southampton at the Dell, manager Alex Ferguson blaming the strip which he claimed made it difficult for players to pick out their team-mates against the background of the crowd. They returned to the fray in more conspicuous shirts — though Ryan Giggs reduced the arrears slightly, the title-chasers failed to get back on terms — and the grey shirts were never seen again.

CHRIS THE CENTURION

BACK WHEN SPORTSMEN could combine careers in cricket and football, Chris Balderstone was the most successful of the breed. Towards the end of his career in the 1970s, when he'd signed for Doncaster Rovers, he batted until close of play at 6.30, then was chauffeured to a Rovers game which kicked off at 7.30! He resumed his innings the following morning and completed a century. He remains associated with cricket to this day as a first-class umpire, but Carlisle fans will recall over 350 games for the Brunton Park side.

The realisation of what it means to be a Manchester City fan.

SUPERSUBS

CHARITY CHEER FOR DAVE

UNLIKE THEIR Merseyside counterparts, Manchester's City and United have only once met in the Charity Shield — and even then it wasn't at Wembley but at Maine Road in October 1956. The game, which United won by a single goal, was memorable for the fact that it saw a rare use of a substitute when Ray Wood, the Red Devils' keeper, was unable to continue after injury. By a gentlemen's agreement between managers, 15 year old Dave Gaskell was able to play the rest of the match — and the schoolboy international proved his potential by keeping a clean sheet! He'd later play in three official derbies.

Psst! Andy! The goal's over here.

A WALK(ER) ON THE NICE SIDE

MANAGER BILLY MCNEILL once said that angels don't win you anything except a place in heaven. Obviously he hadn't heard of a certain Gary Lineker. In 1990 Leicester-born Lineker, the notorious nice guy of football, won FIFA's £20,000 Fair Play award as a result of never being booked or sent off during his career. This also rubbed off on his team-mates, as in the 1986 World Cup England also picked up the Fair Play trophy.

However, there was much more to Gary Lineker than a clean game, as he established himself as one of the world's greatest goalscorers. His success can be effectively summed up in his achievements in 1986, when he scored 30 League goals, was awarded two Player of the Year awards and then went on to become the leading scorer in the World Cup.

Lineker is also England's second leading scorer, one behind Bobby Charlton, on 48 international goals. His long quest to beat that record came to a controversial end in 1992 when he was substituted in a European Championship game against Sweden and never played international football again.

HOW TO SAVE £15 MILLION!

ALAN SHEARER MADE football history when he was transferred from Blackburn Rovers to Newcastle United in July 1996 for a record £15 million. But the Geordies could have had him for nothing had they been a little more alert. Shearer, who lived streets away from St James' Park, had a miniature Magpies kit as a child and wanted nothing more than to play for his local heroes. They ran the rule over him, didn't think he would make the grade and it was left to Southampton scout Jack Hixon to send the youngster south.

Shearer moved on from the Dell to Ewood Park in 1992 for £3.6 million — but another error crept in here when the Saints forgot to have a 'sell-on' clause written in to give them a share of any profit Blackburn would make on any subsequent move. Hence the fat £11 million profit stayed in Lancashire!

> **6** In the north-east as soon as you can walk you're thrown a ball at your feet and they say: 'There you go, kick it!' And I was no different. **9**
>
> ALAN SHEARER

ROYLE BLUES

FANS AT GOODISON Park will readily admit that manager Joe Royle has made great changes at the club, turning the Toffees into a considerable Premiership force — a point underlined with their sixth-place finish in 1995-96.

It's not surprising, then, that many are expecting Royle to start rewriting the record books pretty soon. But few realise that his name already graces the history books at Goodison Park. Back in his younger days, a more sylph-like Royle became the youngest player to appear in a Football League match for Everton. On his debut for the club against Blackpool in January 1966, he was just 16 years and 288 days old.

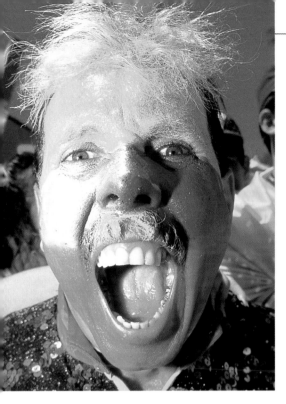

THEY ALL LOOK BLOODY STUPID.

ALL WASHED UP

MANCHESTER CITY have two players, Francis Lee and Joe Hayes, who jointly hold the record of most derby goals scored for their side against Manchester United. Both enter the record books with ten goals apiece. Hayes would, however, have the clear edge had a match between the sides not been abandoned in 1960 with the score 2-2, Hayes having notched one. His fellow scorer Denis Law had even worse luck when his six goals in a match against Luton were similarly washed out: perhaps inevitably, Luton won the replay!

WEATHER OR NOT...

EVER SINCE THE FA Cup kicked off in 1871, it had refused to be beaten by the British weather. Even the notorious 'big freeze' seasons of 1947 and 1963 couldn't prevent at least one game of every round of every year's Cup being played... even if the rest had to be rescheduled. That proud record came to a wet and windy end on 8 February 1969 when the entire eight-match Fifth Round programme failed to take place — an event that pleased only the Pools Panel!

GROUND TO A HALT

ALTHOUGH PLAYERS have a long, relaxing summer vacation, groundsmen across the country spend the finer months frantically repairing their pitches in time for next season when it will start all over again.

This was especially true of Reading's Gordon Neate, when the club gained promotion to the Second Division in 1986. Despite months of work through the close-season the pitch was unsuitable to be played on until Reading were well into their fixture list.

The reason? The unfortunate Mr Neate had apparently used weedkiller on the pitch instead of fertiliser!

SEEING RED

YOU ONLY HAVE to switch on the television on a Saturday afternoon in January to see the most common cause for matches being postponed or abandoned is the weather.

Under today's rules, an abandoned match should be replayed in full — but that hasn't always been the case. For example, in 1888 a match between Sheffield Wednesday and Aston Villa was abandoned with only ten minutes remaining. The two sides then met 15 weeks later to play the remaining ten minutes and 30 seconds.

However, bad weather isn't the only reason for a match to be abandoned. A referee was forced to halt an international between Chile and Uruguay in 1975 because there weren't enough players on the pitch to complete it. This was because he had sent off ten Chileans and nine Uruguayans following a mass fight between the teams!

SPOT THE STAR

IF YOU EVER thought the Pools Panel was a device to give ex-professional footballers something to do on wet Saturday afternoons, then consider the committee that judges Vernons Spot The Ball. This distinguished body grants part-time employment to no fewer than three former Anfield Idols – David Johnson, Phil Thompson and Alan Kennedy. To ensure impartiality, however, Johnson started life with local rivals Everton!

Hands up, all those who think Scotland has a good football team.

CELEBRITY FOOTBALLERS

BEEFY AND THE BIG BALL

INTERNATIONAL CRICKETER Ian Botham filled in his winters when not playing abroad by turning out for local League club Scunthorpe United. Signing for them in 1980, he managed seven League games, plus another four as substitute, until hanging up his boots in 1984, also turning out at non-League level for Yeovil Town. This short period of combining summer and winter sport led to a poser that might even have fooled his fellow competitors on TV's *A Question Of Sport*: name three England captains Scunthorpe United have produced? The others, for the record, are Ray Clemence and Kevin Keegan!

ROY'S ALL DWIGHT!

ELTON JOHN'S INTEREST in football that led him to become chairman of Watford stemmed from his uncle, Roy Dwight, who played for several clubs in his career. He achieved unfortunate fame in 1959 when he broke his leg in the FA Cup Final, sustaining one of the worst injuries the fixture had ever witnessed. A silver lining came – literally – in the shape of a winner's medal when his ten colleagues beat Luton by two goals to nil, the first of which Dwight scored himself. Twenty five years later, Elton was at Wembley with Watford, but the Hornets lost 2-0 to Everton – thankfully with no injury to anything but their pride.

OFF

HOME-GROWN HEROES ONLY!

WHEN HE SIGNED for Manchester City, Gordon Davies was looking forward to playing in a derby against neighbours United. But it was never to be, thanks to an unusual selection policy from manager Billy McNeill. "We were playing United on the Saturday and Chelsea at Wembley in the Full Members Cup Final on the Sunday, so McNeill decided to play all the Manchester born and bred lads because he felt they would put more emphasis on the local derby. The lads who didn't play on the Saturday would be playing on the Sunday.

"So I missed out on the game at Old Trafford — and then was dropped for the game on the Sunday against Chelsea, the team I'd joined City from. It was fun to see their reaction because they all thought I'd be playing. When I told them I wasn't even sub, I think I lifted them because they weren't looking forward to playing against me. I knew them inside-out, and it was a great chance for me to put one over on the club that let me go. To this day I don't know why he left me out."

BUSBY BREAKS THE BANK

MATT BUSBY, Manchester United's greatest manager of all time, never played for the club. Instead, he played for Moss Side neighbours Manchester City, and arrived at Old Trafford via a spell at Anfield as a coach. Yet it's a little-known fact that he could have got there over a decade earlier had United been able to raise £150 to buy him. Even converted into today's values, £150 isn't a lot, but cash-strapped United just couldn't afford to buy the Scottish half-back who remained in a blue shirt — for the moment, anyway!

TALE OF THREE CITIES

ONLY TWO PLAYERS are known to have played in the three major English derby matches. They are Brian Kidd and Paul Walsh, each of whom has played in the Manchester, Merseyside and North London clashes. Interestingly they represented opposing sides — Kidd: Manchester United, Everton and Arsenal, Walsh: City, Liverpool and Spurs — though Kidd also served a spell with City in the late 1970s. He's now Manchester United's assistant manager while Walsh, at Portsmouth, has less fond memories of the Cottonopolis contest. He lost all three he competed in, 2-0, 3-0 and 5-0!

BRUCE ON THE LOOSE

EVERTON SKIPPER Kevin Ratcliffe played in 30 derby games against local rivals Liverpool — but only ever scored one goal, which dribbled into the net from long range back in 1986. And ever since the 'bung' allegations against then-Liverpool keeper Bruce Grobbelaar surfaced, he's had to defend it against jokey allegations that the Zimbabwean was giving him a helping hand!

And quite literally thousands of Russians were there in Red Square to appreciate the wacky antics of England's Chris Woods.

WEMBLEY'S WANT-AWAY

THERE'S NEVER A good time to slap down a transfer request – but Blackburn Rovers' centre-forward Derek Dougan must have chosen a uniquely unusual one when, an hour before his team's 1960 FA Cup Final against Wolves, he approached boss Dally Duncan. As it happened, neither 'Doog' nor his team-mates excelled in a 3-0 loss to Wolves – ironically the team with which he'd find greatest success later in the decade. He knuckled down and stayed more than a year at Ewood Park before leaving for Aston Villa in 1961.

CULTURAL EXCHANGE

WHEN ARGENTINIAN Alberto Tarantini, one of British football's first foreign 'imports', came to play for Birmingham City in the 1970s he made a special friend in Trevor Francis. City's talented young forward taught the newcomer English, so that Tarantini is now one of the few Argentines to speak with a broad Devon accent. In return, he taught Francis's wife Helen how to cook steak South American style – but unfortunately star performances on the pitch were decidedly 'rare', and he returned home soon after.

TO MOVE OR NOT TO MOVE

WHEN NORWICH CITY gave midfield playmaker Ian 'Chippie' Crook a free transfer in the summer of 1996, he was delighted when local rivals Ipswich Town offered him a contract. After all, he could stay in his house, the kids could stay in school... but it was still a wrench to leave. So, when former Norwich boss Mike Walker returned to Carrow Road to take up the reins and offered him a coaching job, it was too good to be true. Unfortunately Crook had already signed... but, because it was still one day before his Norwich contract ran out, managed to move back without ever wearing the blue of Ipswich. Hopefully, both sets of fans – traditionally great rivals – can forgive and forget.

FEES PLEASE!

THERE HAVE BEEN some strange transfer fees changing hands during the history of the game: future Eire international Tony Cascarino, for instance, made the journey from Crockenhill to Gillingham for a set of tracksuits. At the other end of the financial scale, Jimmy Greaves returned to England from Italy in 1961 for £99,999, Tottenham manager Bill Nicholson not wanting his charge to have the burden of the first ever six-figure fee!

> ❛ We used to be lucky to get one man and his dog turning up at training. When Kenny arrived, 400 people turned up. ❜
>
> BLACKBURN ROVERS COACH TONY PARKES ON KENNY DALGLISH

> ❛ We're all pawns in the game, they use you and cast you aside... but hey, life's a bitch! ❜
>
> COVENTRY'S JOHN SALAKO

WHY ARE FOOTBALLERS SO OBSESSED WITH BOGIES?

Referee Mike Reed was so proud, he showed his to Sunderland's David Kelly...

Grobbelaar's was innocent...

and Tottenham's Ian Walker even called in ground staff to protect a particularly fine example....

Colombians habitually keep their nasal habits discreet...

And Barcelona's youth policy shows why they are the phlegm cream of European football.

THE GOOD, THE BAD AND THE WINNERS

ALTHOUGH ENGLAND were unable to lift the winner's trophy in Euro '96 they did manage to win the Fair Play award, thus keeping the country's reputation as a nation that values honour and sportsmanship.

This tradition can be traced as far back as 1875, in the days before the Football League, when England faced their old enemy Scotland in an international in London.

England and Owlerton goalkeeper William Carr had missed his train — and, rather than delay the match until he arrived Charles Alcock, the home captain, nobly decided to start the match with only ten men.

The depleted side managed to hold out until their keeper arrived, 15 minutes into the game, only to see him let two goals in as the match finished 2-2. Neither Carr nor Alcock, who scored England's second, ever played for their country again. It just goes to prove that the 'good guys' don't always win!

ONE FINGER SHORT OF A GLOVE

IT'S WIDELY ACCEPTED in football that goalkeepers are eith exceedingly brave, or are just plain silly. One example of such 'brave can be seen in the efforts of Bert Trautmann, the Manchester Ci goalkeeper, during the FA Cup Final of 1956 against Birmingham City. On two occasions Trautmann rushed to the feet of oncoming forwar and both times he was injured. In the first incident he was knocked o after receiving heavy hits to his head and neck, and five minutes lat a second challenge knocked him to the floor again. He picked hims up and managed to play the remaining 15 minutes of the game Manchester City won 3-1.

Three days later Trautmann was taken to hospital after complaining headaches. X-rays were taken and they found the cause of Ber discomfort. During the match the German-born keeper had broken neck, yet somehow managed to play on!

RUSH GOALIES

INJURIES AND SUSPENSIONS were rife in Euro '96, to such an extent that Germany, the competition's winners, put both substitute goalkeepers into outfield shirts in case they should be called upon to take part in play. Peter Schmeichel of Manchester United often comes upfield at the end of games for free-kicks and corners to try to score — and did so in the 1995 UEFA Cup tie against Rotor Volgograd. He's not the first United keeper to try his hand at scoring: Alex Stepney notched two penalties for the club in the 1973-74 season.

"Yeah it's great to meet you and such a surprise to see you doin this. My favourite? Oh that would have to be 'So You Win Again'

Never mind me. You should see the Swedes!

NEVER TOO OLD

THEY SAY GOALKEEPERS have a longer life than outfield players – but Ronnie Simpson certainly found things going his way late in life. He joined Celtic at the advanced age of 34, and certainly couldn't have realised that he'd be picking up a European Cup winner's medal three years later. Scotland, too, honoured him, awarding the first of five caps in 1967 when he was 36.

GREAT GUNNER

ARSENAL STRIKER Malcolm Macdonald freely admits that he didn't rate goalkeeper Pat Jennings until they both arrived at Highbury because he always seemed to score goals against him. "Once he signed with Arsenal the only time I went against him was in training, and he had this horrible habit in shooting practice. You'd make your shot and he'd stand there, not moving, and go 'post'... Sure enough, the ball would hit the post and come out. Another time you'd take a shot, he wouldn't move and he'd say 'bar' and it would hit the bar and come out. He was unfailing in that."

KEEP GOING, KEEPER

THERE ARE A number of things that have always been part of football and it seems likely that they always will. For example, the ball, the goals, the pitch and... Neville Southall. The Welsh goalkeeper made his Football League debut in 1980 for Bury and since then has spent most of his time at Everton. Not only has he made nearly 700 appearances for the Goodison outfit, a club record which no one is able to challenge, but he also holds the record for the most seasons without missing a game: a staggering five. He also holds the Welsh record for the most international caps, at present approaching the century mark.

NICE TO SEE YOU!

KNOWN UNIVERSALLY AS 'Budgie', John Burridge is the most travelled goalkeeper in English football history. While a member of Newcastle United's coaching staff he would help out other injury-hit clubs as a player. Ironically he kept a clean sheet against his employers in April 1995 while in Manchester City's colours, at the age of 43 – becoming the Premiership's oldest player in the process!

NINE PAST HAFFEY

THE MYTH OF Scottish goalkeepers so beloved by Jimmy Greaves probably stems back to his playing days when he was one of the England side that thrashed the Scots 9-3 in 1962. The keeper who had to bend his back more often than most was Celtic's Frank Haffey – a happy-go-lucky character who, fortunately, took the event as the freak it was, rather than a career-destroying performance.

Haffey, who later emigrated to Australia to pursue a career as a cabaret singer, didn't please his team-mates, though, by later posing for the papers in front of a clock with the hands at nine and three. And the joke that went the rounds for many a month between English and Scots was: "What's the time?" "Nine past Haffey!"

A TALE OF TWO KEEPERS

TWO LONDON GOALKEEPERS, now residing in America, have different memories FA Cup Finals. Peter Mellor, now the state of Florida's goalkeeping coac undoubtedly tells his charges not to do what he did in the 1975 Cup Final and let in through his legs! The opponents that day were West Ham, for whom Jim Stande won an FA Cup medal in 1964. Now resident in California, he also coaches, and h the car number plate FA CUP 64 to remind him of past glories. Incidentally, t Fulham-West Ham Final was 'replayed' in 1995 with most of the original playe Fulham won this time, 2-1... but Mellor still let one in through his legs!

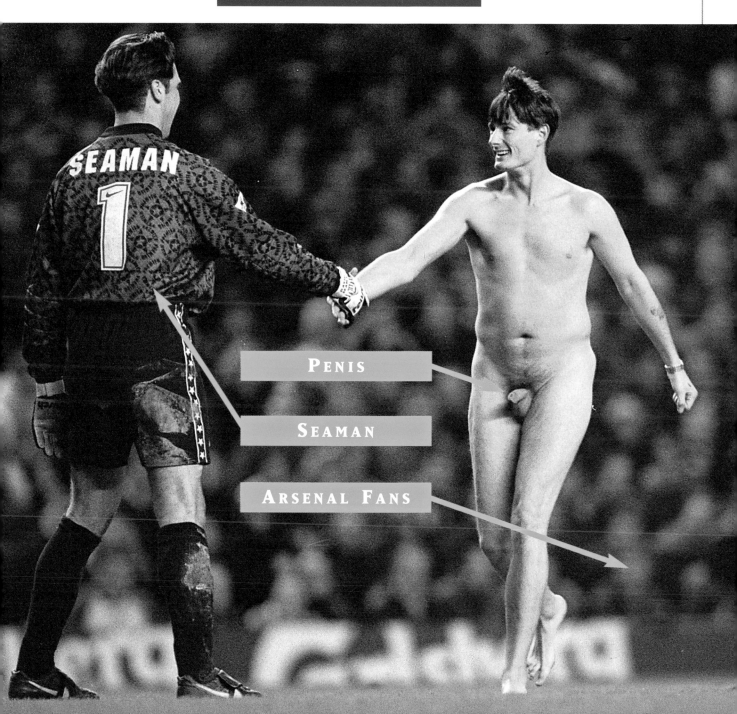

PENIS

SEAMAN

ARSENAL FANS

FOOTBALL ISN'T JUST A MATTER OF LIFE AND DEATH...

GIBSON'S GOLDEN GAFFE

EVERY PLAYER HAS his off day. For some, it happens in front of a couple of thousand at a soccer outpost like Spotland or Saltergate, while others are unfortunate enough to play their 'mare' (as professionals call it) in the glare of publicity and television coverage. Davie Gibson can certainly empathise with that: his disastrous moment came in the 1963 Cup Final against mighty Manchester United while playing with Leicester.

Keeper Gordon Banks bowled the ball out to him, but his failure to control it left Pat Crerand in possession — and his cross found the deadly Denis Law with predictable results. The goal, and the gaffe, has been shown on television so many times that Gibson's children have started giving him stick: "You've been trying to trap that ball for 20 years," they've said, "and you still can't manage it!"

SHOCKING!

IN A COMPETITIVE sport such as football, injuries and accidents are not uncommon — and more than one career has been brought to an end because of a broken leg.

Thankfully, fatalities are rare but not unheard of. Most of those who have died have done so some time after their last match as a result of their injuries.

However, there have been those who have died during a match, and many of these have been in curious circumstances. James Beaumont died in 1877, while playing a match in Sheffield, when he fell into a quarry next to the pitch.

Tragedies also occur on the continent, such as the case of a Spanish player who was electrocuted when he picked up a live cable which had fallen onto the pitch.

THERE'S ALWAYS TO-MORROW

THE LEAGUE CUP Final of 1993 was a day of mixed emotions for Arsenal's Steve Morrow. Having scored the winning goal in Arsenal's 2-1 defeat of Sheffield Wednesday, Morrow was on a high as the Gunners paraded themselves and the trophy in front of their supporters at Wembley.

Rather than lift the Cup above his head Tony Adams, the Arsenal captain, decided that he would place goal hero Morrow on his shoulders. Unfortunately, the player weighed a bit more than the trophy and Adams dropped him. Steve Morrow broke his arm in the fall which meant that he was unable to play in that season's FA Cup Final! Arsenal went on to win the FA Cup, beating Sheffield Wednesday once again by the same score, 2-1.

LET THERE BE LIGHT!

THE FIRST OFFICIAL Football League match to be played under floodlights was in 1956 at Fratton Park, the home of Portsmouth, and saw visiting Newcastle beat the home side 2-0.

The idea of floodlights had been around for many years, but the FA had strongly resisted calls for League games to be played under these conditions. It even went as far as banning member clubs from playing any matches under floodlights after 1930.

The first recorded match ever to take place under floodlights was in 1878 and took place at Bramall Lane, now the home of Sheffield United. The lighting system at this time used oil rather than electricity which resulted in a high risk of fire and an unpleasant smell.

THAT CAPS IT ALL!

WHEN CELTIC completed a record 7-1 win in the 1957 Scottish League Cup Final against local rivals Rangers, it was broadcast in highlight form later that day — but unfortunately only the first half was able to be viewed. (The score at half-time was 2-0.) A technician filming the pictures, had forgotten to take the lens cap off his camera after his half-time break!

Celtic chief Jock Stein would rib BBC Scotland commentator Archie McPherson — not the man responsible — after any subsequent victory by his team with the words "Did you get the dust cover off the camera this time?"

OOH

AAH

CANTON-AAH

GOALS GALORE

3 IS THE MAGIC NUMBER

SCORING A HAT-TRICK is a truly great achievement – and few are more memorable than Geoff Hurst's three goals against Germany in the World Cup Final of 1966.

The sharpest of goalscorers, though, must surely be Dixie Dean, a man still regarded by many as the best centre-forward England has ever produced. His record of 37 hat-tricks in the Football League between 1923-37 still stands despite today's multi-million pound strikers. How much would Dixie be worth in today's game?

The record for the quickest hat-trick in British football belongs to Jock Dodds of Blackpool, who took just two and a half minutes to score three goals against Tranmere in 1943.

The term hat-trick is borrowed from the cricketing tradition that if a bowler took three wickets in succession he was entitled to a new hat which was to be paid for by the club. In football, the player is allowed to keep the match ball.

WINDOW SHOPPING ON SCREEN

AS EUROPEAN IMPORTS into the Premiership gathered pace in the mid 1990s, managers started to shop for prospective purchasers. Some, though, went further than others while the smarter bosses did their talent-spotting from the comfort of their own front rooms. Leeds' Howard Wilkinson invested in a satellite dish... and was rewarded by spotting Tony Yeboah slotting them in for Eintracht Frankfurt in the Bundesliga. Over at Villa Park, Brian Little was impressed with what he saw of striker Savo Milosevic on a video cassette his agent supplied – but so poorly did the striker play in the first part of his debut season the fans reckoned the highlights were severely edited! (To his credit, though, he topped the second half with an unforgettable Wembley goal.)

> 6 Football has given me riches, popularity and privileges but i want even more. I live for undescribable emotions – and football can give me those. 9
>
> CHELSEA'S GIANLUCA VIALLI

> 6 It's the thrill of scoring goals that makes me play football... satisfaction, joy and occasionally, relief, all rolled into a few seconds of pure ecstasy. 9
>
> GARY LINEKER

COMMUNICATION GAP

WITH THREE SPANIARDS joining Wigan in 1995, foreign imports have made an impression at all levels of the League game. Not least in a club that shall remain nameless where the manager, after a run of fruitless games, went back to first principles. 'Ball' he pronounced, gesturing to the sphere, before moving on to 'goal' and 'score' as he kicked one through the other. "I think they knew that already, boss," remarked his cynical captain of the watching foreigners. "It's not them I'm worried about," retorted the harassed manager. "I'm talking to the rest of you!"

See Frank, I told
ya Arsenal played
entertaining soccer.

SEND ON THE PHYSIO

HUNTING THE HARD MEN

MUCH HAS BEEN made of today's 'hard men of football' such as Vinnie Jones and Julian Dicks, but one shouldn't forget the ironically named Norman 'Bites Yer Legs' Hunter.

Hunter, who played for Leeds and England, is regarded by many as the strongest tackler the game has ever seen. Despite his crunching tackles and fearsome reputation Hunter proved he was more than a hard man by being the first player to win the PFA's Player of the Year award in 1973.

His England and Leeds trainer, Les Cocker, recalls one occasion when Hunter phoned him to say that he had gone home with a broken leg. Cocker replied: "Whose leg is it?"

Jim Baxter once said, 'great players are great boozers',
and he was right. Most of them are.
GEORGE BEST

On our bad days we couldn't win a fight with a midget.
JOE ROYLE ON FORMER CLUB OLDHAM

6 Colin is one of those guys who isn't happy unless he's
been kicked in the bollocks three times in training. 9

GRAEME LE SAUX ON TEAM-MATE COLIN HENDRY

6.0

6.0

6.0

5.9

6.0

5.9

OFF

THEY'RE PLAYING OUR SONG...

A JOURNEYMAN centre-half with a sense of humour that arguably exceeded his talent, Londoner Terry Mancini enjoyed an Indian summer at Arsenal. There he came to the notice of Eire, who soon found an Irish relative to assure him a place in the national side. He was standing at Lansdowne Road, chest puffed out with pride, when the anthems were played, but found the formalities a little tiresome. "I wish they'd get a move on with their anthem – it goes on for ages," he reportedly commented to a team-mate. "Shut up, Terry," came the whispered response. "It's ours!"

POLICE PREDICTION

WITH HIS FAMOUS team of the 1960s already fading, Bill Shankly was keen to secure the cornerstone of a new dynasty in Blackpool teenager Emlyn Hughes. His pursuit of the player was accelerated by the departure of the Bloomfield Road manager, so he sped to complete the signing before the incomer could change his mind or hike the price up. Then, still fuelled by elation, he drove Hughes back to Anfield – only to be stopped for speeding. As the traffic cop looked him up and down, Shankly, unperturbed, bade Hughes leave the car and announced, proudly, 'Officer, look at this boy. He is a future captain of England!' As ever, Shankly would eventually be proved right – and he got off with a lecture!

SWOPPING SHIRTS

WITH PARENTAL qualifications seeming to qualify anyone to play for anyone else these days, it's interesting to note that certain names could have appeared on different international team sheets. Ryan Giggs, for instance, appeared for England at schoolboy level before deciding to represent Wales. By contrast, Wrexham-born Rob Jones wore the red shirt of the Principality as a child before hopping over the border to represent England. He also switched life at Gresty Road, Crewe, for a dressing-room peg at Anfield, but that's another story...

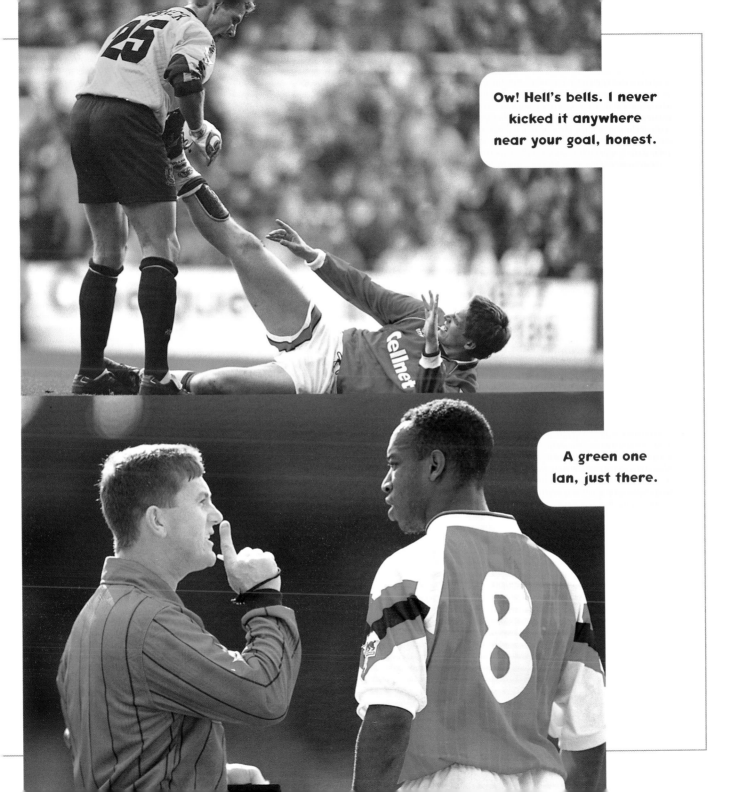

Answer: Vinnie Jones.

WHAT'S IN A NAME?

ANOTHER CLUB, ANOTHER PLANET

FANZINES HAVE BORROWED their names from some weird and wonderful sources over the years. Rangers chose the title of their traditional chant *Follow Follow*, while an ex-Rangers striker titled Brighton's *And Smith Must Score*, named after his FA Cup Final gaffe in 1983. Others are plays on words, like *There's Only One F In Fulham*, that need to be heard to be understood. But perhaps the funniest is *Brian Moore's Head Looks Uncannily Like London Planetarium*, an observation on the features of the veteran Gillingham supporter (and sometime director) who has commentated on ITV for many a year.

A VERY BRITISH BOBBY

FOOTBALLERS TEND TO keep unusual names a secret. Some which deserve a wider audience though include Primrose, the middle name of Arsenal keeper turned TV presenter Bob Wilson and Euclid Aklana, the middle monickers of Tottenham's Clive Wilson. Clive's team-mate Sol Campbell's real christian name is Sulzeer, while Bolton's ex-Spur Chris Fairclough is really Calvin. His former Leeds team-mate John Lukic was born Jovan Lukic, while Reading's Bulgarian keeper Boris Mikhailov decided to change his first name to Bobby, thinking it more British. So did Andrea Silenzi who on signing for Nottingham Forest decided he'd rather be called Andy – for purely masculine reasons!

DIVINE INTERVENTION

RAISING SPIRITS

IF LEYTON ORIENT'S players are feeling unhappy, depressed or even suicidal after a run of bad results, then they can quite literally take Comfort! Alan Comfort, a flying winger who not only served the Brisbane Road club as well as Cambridge and Middlesbrough, was forced to retire from the game through injury in his mid-20s. He decided to take up holy orders and as well as being minister of St Chad's, Chadwell Heath, he is also club chaplain for the O's. He's written a book on his conversion from player to pastor, in which he compares his experiences with Chelsea's Gavin Peacock, another committed Christian.

ALL NOADES LEAD TO...

THE CAREERS OF John Leslie and Dave Bassett first crossed when both played for Wimbledon, then the League's newest club. 'Harry' Bassett, then a part-time insurance agent, sold Leslie the policy with which he bought his house – but more was to come. The pair actually spent Leslie's wedding night together in a Huddersfield hotel! Having got married the day before a game, John and his room-mate were driven up to Yorkshire in then-chairman Ron Noades' Rolls-Royce.

SIGNS OF THE TIMES

DURING THE 1960s, the pastor at a small Christian Mission hall just outside Liverpool's Anfield Road ground had the habit of putting up stirring messages or bible texts to catch the eye of the passing masses – alas, a rather larger number on alternate Saturdays than passed through his doors on a Sunday.

One week, the message read: "What will you do when Jesus comes to Liverpool?" Underneath this, a passing wag had added the solution: "Move St John to inside-left!" It's also rumoured the same man doctored a later slogan that read: "Jesus saves – but Keegan nets the rebound"...

‘ I'm not a believer in luck, although I do believe you need it. ’

ALAN BALL

DIVE! DIVE! DIVE!

HE MAY HAVE left as the reigning Footballer of the Year, but German striker Jürgen Klinsmann's shock arrival in the Premiership in 1994 wasn't greeted with approval by all. 'Sinsman Klinsmann' was just one of the headlines suggesting that the blond bomber had 'taken a dive' or two in the course of procuring penalties with club and country. Referees were told to look out for such Continental 'conning'.

But crafty Klinsmann had the last laugh. After scoring the winner at Sheffield Wednesday in his first game, he ran joyously towards the Tottenham fans and spreadeagled himself in the most spectacular dive seen since the last Olympics. His delighted team-mates followed suit!

> 6 it has been a tremendous week for me. First the MBE, a goal in the reserves after a cartilage operation and now Denis Law's record. i was so pleased it happened at Anfield and particularly at the Kop end. 9
>
> LIVERPOOL'S IAN RUSH

DUCKING THE ISSUE!

EVERY YEAR THE BBC's Road To Wembley follows the progress of non-League hopefuls as they aim to meet the big boys. Aylesbury United, coming from a town famous for its ducks, were 'fair game', so to speak, having made their way through the qualifying rounds to the competition proper in the 1994-95 season.

After a while, they decided to get their own back and rehearsed one of the most unusual mass celebrations ever, dropping to their knees and 'waddling' the length of the pitch duck style. Sadly, they ended up scoreless and 'stuffed' against QPR.

SAME NAME, SAME STYLE

RICARDO VILLA AND Roger Milla are similar names - and the Argentine and Cameroon stars both hit the headlines with their style of celebration. In the 1981 Cup Final replay, Villa capped one of the greatest goals Wembley had seen in living memory, a mazy run that left several Manchester City defenders flat out in his wake by a burst of speed that challenged his own team-mates to catch him!

Veteran striker Milla, meanwhile, was everybody's hit of the 1990 World Cup with his style of jiving with the corner flag to mark a goal. Sadly for him, England's quarter-final victory brought those celebrations to a premature end.

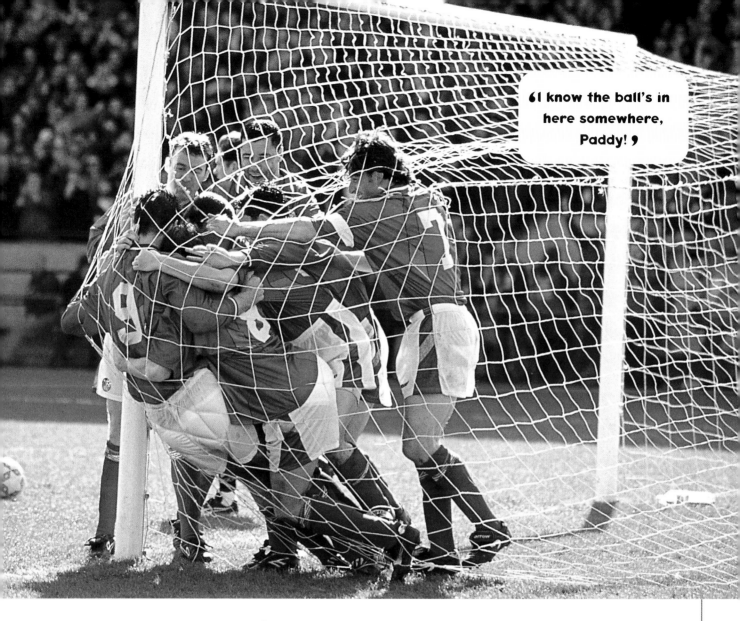

‘I know the ball's in here somewhere, Paddy!’

GORDAN GETS SHIRTY

RANGERS STOPPER Gordan Petric is known for his efficiency rather than his entertainment value. But all that changed when, after scoring their third goal against Vladikavkaz in August 1996, the big Serbian ripped off his shirt and swung it around his head! Unfortunately the referee didn't see the joke and booked Petric. The team's comeback in this qualifying game after going 1-0 down suggested they'd 'booked' a place in the European Cup proper.

SHARPE'S A SMOOTH MOVER

WHEN ELVIS 'THE PELVIS' Presley first appeared on TV, cameramen had orders to cut him off at the waist (so to speak) in case his hip-swivelling should incite a nation's youth. Three decades or more later, Lee Sharpe - then of Manchester United, now at Leeds - had the same effect as he and fellow glamour boy Ryan Giggs brought more young ladies into Old Trafford than the Theatre Of Dreams had seen since George Best's heyday. The Sharpe Shuffle, a bump'n'grind routine that would merit at least a PG certificate if shown on the big screen, soon made *Match Of The Day* a must-see for a generation of girls as well as boys!

> ❝ People will look at me and think I'm not enjoying it but it was fantastic. I'm every bit as happy as the fellows. ❞
>
> MANAGER BRIAN LITTLE
> AFTER ASTON VILLA'S 1996
> COCA-COLA CUP FINAL TRIUMPH.

PAUL KNOWS THE DRILL

THE KNIVES WERE out for Paul 'Gazza' Gascoigne and his team-mates when their pre-Euro '96 drinking spree in a Hong Kong nightclub was brought to light. Followed by allegations of further high jinks on an air flight back home, the side entered a competition they had high hopes of winning on a decidedly downbeat note.

But Clown Prince Gazza had something up his sleeve for when he scored his first goal, a cracker against the Old Enemy Scotland at Wembley. A carefully choreographed routine saw two team-mates hoist him off the turf as others squirted drinks canisters at him, copying the infamous dentist's chair ritual that had caused the furore. The bevvies were non-alcoholic this time, but England ended the match, if not the tournament, on a high.

OFF BALL

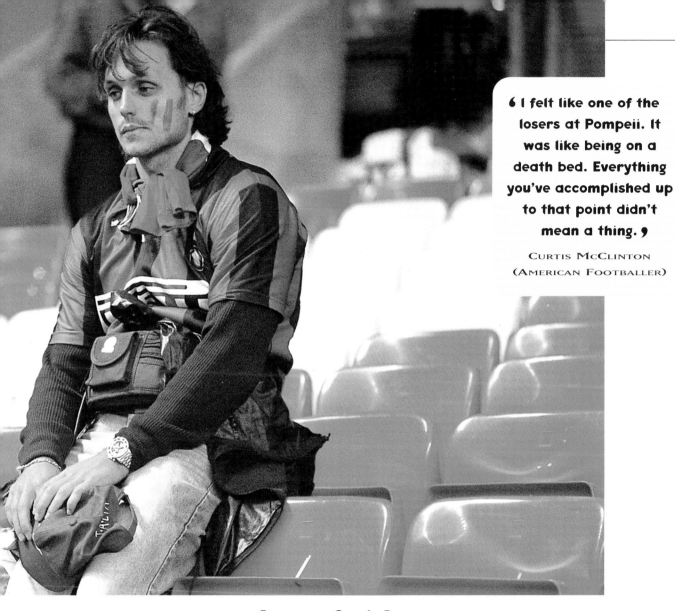

> **' I felt like one of the losers at Pompeii. It was like being on a death bed. Everything you've accomplished up to that point didn't mean a thing. '**
>
> CURTIS MCCLINTON
> (AMERICAN FOOTBALLER)

LEAVING ON A JETPLANE

WHEN HE ARRIVED at Swindon Town from Rapid Vienna in 1993, Norwegian international Jan Aage Fjortoft was expected to score goals. What the County Ground crowd didn't anticipate was his tendency to celebrate them as if trying to get airborne! This jetplane style activity seems to have caught on and with Mikkel Beck, another Scandinavian considering joining Fjortoft at Middlesbrough in 1996, the Teesside crowd will be hoping a Championship challenge takes off.

Q: Fabrizio Ravanelli/Juventus

A: Paul Gascoigne/Rangers

A: Luis Enrique/Spain

A: Brian Deane/Leeds

OFF

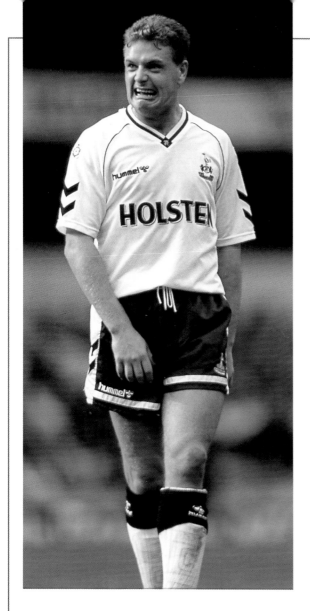

> ❛ He is accused of being arrogant, unable to cope with the press, and a boozer. Sounds like he's got a chance to me. ❜
>
> GEORGE BEST

❝ Football people may tell you about the skills and the beauty of the game, and we know they exist, but don't let's kid ourselves; most people go to a football game for the violence. ❞

DR THOMAS TUTKO
(SPORTS PSYCHOLOGIST)

❝ I don't watch TV myself. But my family do and they tell me the most popular programmes are the ones which are full of violence. On that basis football ought to do rather well. ❞

JACK DUNNETT
PRESIDENT OF THE
FOOTBALL LEAGUE

OFF

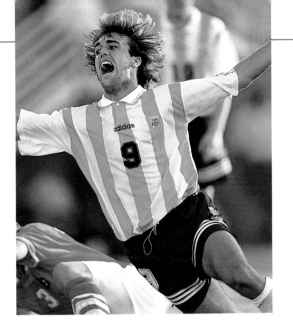

> **6 Norman Hunter
> does not tackle
> opponents so
> much as break
> them down for
> resale as scrap. 9**
>
> JULIE WELCH

> **6 I have a little black book
> with two players in it, and if
> I get a chance to do them I will.
> I will make them suffer before I
> pack this game in. if I can kick
> them four yards over the
> touch-line, I will. 9**
>
> JACK CHARLTON

‘ Football, in itself, is a
grand game for developing a
lad physically and also
morally, for he learns to play
with good temper and
unselfishness, to play in his
place and 'play the game'…
But it is a vicious game
when it draws crowds of lads
away from playing
the game themselves to be
merely onlookers at a few
paid performers. ’

LORD BADEN-POWELL

The Chairman says the Board is 100% behind me.

Look at it! Look at it! It's round and it's still. It can't move an inch until someone touches it, so don't talk to me about the run of the ball.

GEORGE SMITH

As a manager, Alf Ramsey is like a good chicken farmer. If a hen doesn't lay, a good chicken farmer wrings its neck.

JACKIE MILBURN

When the FA get in their stride, they make the Mafia look like kindergarden material.

BRIAN CLOUGH

Preston? They're one of my old clubs. But then most of them are. I've had more clubs than Jack Nicklaus.

TOMMY DOCHERTY

It wasn't so much the death threats or the vandalism, but when you sit with your family in the Director's Box and hear a couple of thousand chanting, 'Gilbert Blades is a wanker!' then you feel it's time to resign.

GILBERT BLADES

You're not a real manager unless you've been sacked.

MALCOLM ALLISON

‘ Football is a simple game made unnecessarily complicated by managers. ’

THE PHOTOGRAPHERS

ACTION IMAGES
pages 6, 7, 8, 11, 16, 19, 36, 38, 39, 57, 58, 59, 62, 63, 67, 71, 74, 75, 76, 77, 79, 81, 89, 91, 92, 93, 97, 101, 102, 110, 111,

ALLSPORT PICTURE LIBRARY
pages 55, 65, 106, 107
Ben Radford pages 23, 31, 47, 50
Simon Bruty pages 69, 103
Shaun Botterill page 49
Clive Brumskill page 52
David Cannon page 107
Chris Cole page 27
Phil Cole page 103
Jonathon Daniel page 83
Chris Raphael page 85
Rick Stewart page 106

ACTION PLUS
Chris Barry pages 14, 82
Mike Hewitt pages 104, 105
Jason Shillingford page 105
Tony Henshaw page 53
Glyn Kirk page 99

SPORTS PHOTO AGENCY
Graham Whitby pages 22, 104, 105
James McCauley page 51

MARK LEECH
pages 18, 20, 25, 28, 33, 34, 35, 37, 40, 42, 43, 45, 52, 53, 61, 76, 83, 84, 85, 87, 91, 95,

COVER PHOTOGRAPH:
Sporting Pictures [U.K] Ltd.

OFF
BALL